Haunted Pubs in Devon

Sally and Chips Barber

OBELISK PUBLICATIONS

SOME OTHER TITLES FROM OBELISK

Dark and Dastardly Dartmoor, *Sally and Chips Barber*
Ghastly and Ghostly Devon, *Sally and Chips Barber*
Weird and Wonderful Dartmoor, *Sally and Chips Barber*
The Ghosts of Exeter, *Sally and Chips Barber*
The Ghosts of Torbay, *Deryck Seymour*
The Ghosts of Berry Pomeroy Castle, *Deryck Seymour*
The Ghosts of Totnes, *Bob Mann*
The Ghosts of Brixham, *Graham Wyley*
The Ghosts of Plymouth, *Nancy Hammonds*
Haunted Happenings in Devon, *Judy Chard*
Murders and Mysteries in Devon, *Ann James*
(Films & TV programmes) Made in Devon, *Chips Barber & David FitzGerald*
More Cobblestones, Cottages and Castles, *David Young*
Cobblestones, Cottages and Castles III, *David Young*

We have over 140 Devon titles – for a full list please send an SAE to
Obelisk Publications, 2 Church Hill, Pinhoe, Exeter, EX4 9ER or tel (01392) 468556

Plate Acknowledgements

All drawings by Jane Reynolds
Cover picture by Jane Reynolds
All other photographs by or belonging to Chips Barber

First published in 1995, reprinted in 1996 by
Obelisk Publications, 2 Church Hill, Pinhoe, Exeter, Devon
Designed by Chips and Sally Barber
Typeset by Sally Barber
Printed in Great Britain by
The Devonshire Press Limited, Torquay, Devon

Haunted Pubs in Devon

INTRODUCTION

There's nothing like a good ghost story and if you can manage to throw in, for good measure, a pleasant pub into the bargain, then you can't be far off the mark from what some may deem to be a near 'Utopian' situation – as long as you don't have to greet the ghost personally!

This book is packed with haunted hotels and phantom-populated pubs. However, although we probably won't have you reaching for a little something to help you sleep at night, having read this book, you will, hopefully, enjoy and be fascinated by a range of hauntings from the length and breadth of the county.

If you accept the premise that one person in ten sees or encounters some form of supernatural experience, at some stage of their life, then the same logic should mean that also about one pub in every ten is haunted. Even if this proposed probability is disputed by mathematicians, or even worse, landlords, this little book shows that many have their 'regulars' who take little notice of opening hours!

For convenience the book has been arranged in alphabetical order by the names of the pubs or hotels and not by the places, towns or villages in which they are located so if you try to visit them all in order you will find yourselves crisscrossing the county many times!

AWLISCOMBE INN, AWLISCOMBE

Perhaps this is not the best way to start a book of haunted pubs as, to our knowledge, this pub isn't haunted, yet! However, the first time I (Chips) went there was early one Spring evening, when I strolled into this pub causing the two male customers and barmaid almost to jump out of their skins in fright. It transpired that they had been talking about ghosts and other spooky occurrences, and they were so engrossed in their conversation, that my sudden appearance had caused them to react as if I were a ghost! I was able to tell them something about other ghostly experiences but had to beg their leave just as it was getting to be quite interesting. They were, tickled pink, or was it grey, when they heard that I was due to be just fifty yards away at the village hall to give the members of the WI a talk … about ghosts. That must be the one occasion where the best scare was reserved for those who least expected it!

BAY HORSE, ASHBURTON

Not a lot is known about the various ghosts that have made 'appearances' at this seventeenth century pub in North Street – children have been heard running along an upstairs corridor, and a young girl, believed to have died after contracting diphtheria, has been heard sobbing in an upstairs room.

The pub should really be haunted by the ghosts of departed sailors for this was an inn where they often stayed whilst en route between the ports at the northern and southern extremities of Devon. Their cross-country trek, which took them through Ashburton, was undertaken because the journey around the southwest peninsular was often dangerous and took several days. If they left a ship at Dartmouth and were due to take another at Bideford then they walked overland.

Although the Bay Horse doesn't oblige with maritime spirits, try looking under 'N' for the Northmore Arms at Wonson, near Throwleigh, farther north on the route of the former sailor safari, now referred to as the Mariners' Way.

BAY HORSE INN, TOTNES

This inn is in Cistern Street at the top end of Totnes and its ghost must not be mistaken for some ancient, long-in-the-tooth, former Butlins' entertainer for his distinctive ghostly garb includes a brightly coloured red coat. The late Harold Hall kept this five-hundred-year-old inn. One night, after all but one of the customers had gone home, he chatted in the bar with his sole companion who pointed out to the landlord that there was someone else still there. Harold turned around, had a look but assured the man that there was nobody there. Then Mrs Hall asked the customer if the

person was wearing a red coat, to which the response was "Yes." The landlady casually replied, "That's our ghost!"

BEARSLAKE INN, NEAR BRIDESTOWE

This attractive pub/licensed restaurant is on the main road from Tavistock to Okehampton and lies beneath the high northwestern shoulder of Dartmoor. Although it's an ancient building it hasn't been a pub for very many years.

The pub, where the emphasis is on its restaurant and fine food, has had an unusual progression to reach this status. In the 1960s the owner became mildly irritated by the

large number of cars that pulled up outside for one of its passengers to get out and photograph the building. In a flash of inspiration, the owner thought to herself that here was the perfect opportunity to trade on the quaintness and attractiveness of the property by offering cream teas. This she did, successfully, for several years but eventually she sold the property and it progressed from cream teas into a fully-fledged restaurant and wine bar.

But it was the guests who stayed overnight who were most likely to encounter its rather sad ghost. Apparently 'room 2' is haunted by the ghost of another little girl, sobbing. The young girls who worked here gave her the name 'Mary' as they felt that it fitted with the image they had of her. When the door is opened the noise of her pitiful weeping stops. It has been suggested that having been put to bed to recuperate from an accident, she got out of bed and fell down the stairs, dying soon after from this further crop of injuries.

A few years ago a television crew visited the inn and brought with them a medium. The idea was to allow this person to wander around the premises to see what she could feel or sense. She had no prior knowledge but located the right part of the building. She informed them that the poor, sobbing girl was not 'Mary' but was most definitely 'Kathy'. And there have been many other visitors and guests who have also sensed a definite presence.

BELL INN, CULLOMPTON

This pub lies on the left hand side of the road from Exeter into Cullompton which, not surprisingly, is Exeter Road. The inn was called The Three Chimneys in the past, but for more than a century has been known as The Bell, which gives it a rather familiar ring!

The pub entertains two ghosts and, apparently, nobody has yet called time on these spirits. One is a former landlord who has been seen walking through the bar, many years after his death. The other is believed to be the mother of a former landlady, who was always known as 'Queenie'. This second ghost is known as 'The Green Lady,' almost as colourful, perhaps, as the proverbial 'Pink Elephant.' There is a certain upstairs window that she has been seen through on a number of occasions.

BELL INN, MORETONHAMPSTEAD

Do you have a whipping boy in your household? We are referring to that poor person at whom the finger of blame is pointed whenever something goes awry. The 'ghost' of The Bell Inn falls into this category for a previous landlord's name is used whenever something happens, usually upstairs where meetings are held, requiring a culprit to shoulder the blame. Should you need to call on his services the name to recall, for this perennial scapegoat, is 'Jim Letts'.

THE BISHOP LACY, CHUDLEIGH

The Bishop Lacy at Chudleigh has already featured in *Haunted Happenings in Devon* but there have been many more ghostly presences at this ancient inn, named after a former Bishop of Exeter, Bishop Lacey (yes, with an 'e'!), which continue to add to the pub's haunted reputation.

Do you know what a beer engine is? It's that upright handle that the barman draws slowly back to fill the awaiting beer glass. It's the one customers watch with such great anticipation as their favourite brew fills to a fine head, a pre-whistle whetting wait and they tend to require a degree of muscle to be pulled. In the bar of the Bishop Lacy there is such a beer engine that releases Bass when the thirsty punter demands a quaff of ale. However, this particular one either has a mind of its own or is pulled by a ghost. One early evening, in 1994, when there were just four regulars supping their ale in the bar, they were all rooted to the spot as they saw the lever pull itself back to 'pull a pint'. Knowing the force needed to set it off, they were dumbstruck by the spectacle.

Animals, and dogs in particular, are usually sensitive to the presence of spirits and the son of a former landlord recalled an occasion when unaccountable noises were heard from the upper storey of the pub. The resident Alsation was far from willing to go for a closer encounter, but his owners insisted and the reluctant guard dog was bundled up the stairs. There was nothing and nobody to be seen, but to be on the safe side they shut the door on the dog and waited a few minutes. When they went back to let it out, the poor animal was cowering under the bed!

We have found that virtually all the previous landlords have had some sort of strange experience and quite a few of the regulars had tales to tell as well. As recently as 1995 the landlady, of just a few months, was awakened in the wee small hours as she slept beside her husband. She saw, leaning over him, a 'white' lady, from her long Victorian dress to her whiter than white hair. Despite being seen, she didn't rush away but straightened up, remained for several seconds, then faded away. Perhaps she just likes to check on new residents, for she didn't seem threatening at all.

THE BLAGDON INN, PAIGNTON

This pub is found in the hills on the outskirts of Paignton, beside the road that leads to Totnes. It's red earth Devon at its most vivid and when heavy rains fall (something never mentioned in tourist brochures), the lanes run red in spectacular fashion. The inn benefits from its location in the heartland of all the camping and caravan parks that also populate these hills in the summer season.

The pub's ghost must be taken seriously for it has a very sensitive streak running through it. 'John Henry' as he has been called, has managed to make the headlines of a regional newspaper before and those who live in Paignton should be familiar with this sad spectre.

If you go back a century or two this inn would have been much more of an isolated hostelry than of late. It had stables, stable lads and a groom. This was our friend John Henry. For some unknown reason he decided to end it all. He went into the stables, hitched a rope to a beam and hanged himself.

Since that tragic episode, John Henry has been blamed for a catalogue of incidents, some as minor as moving objects, others as serious as starting a blaze, causing extensive damage. Contemporary reports suggest that a local comedian had referred to John Henry in his routine, the suggestion being that the ghost was so incensed about being ridiculed that he caused the fire. Bet that didn't look too convincing on the insurance claim!

BURRATOR INN, DOUSLAND

Part of this pub was originally Dousland's post office but it closed in 1959 and is now where pool and darts are played. However, don't expect to find the ghost of any postmaster or mistress despatching stamps or any of the other benefits that are doled out at such places. Nor will you find any ghost trains, even though the railway, from Yelverton up to Princetown, used to trundle past its back door on its tortuously twisting journey around the contours to the highest town in England.

The ghosts that frequent this large public house again are more likely to trouble staying, paying guests than its regular patrons. They will need to be on their mettle for an encounter with a lady in black is on the cards. You will know when you see her for she clanks and chinks with the sounds of keys dangling from her person. There is also said to be the ghost of a poor baby who was supposedly murdered here when the pub was a relatively new building (built 1880) that has given the upstairs rooms an eerie feel at times.

CHURCH HOUSE INN, HARBERTON

Harberton is a pretty village, somewhat off the beaten track, just a few miles over the hills to the southwest of Totnes. In fact, because it's off the main road, several writers of guide books about Devon have often left the village out completely. Its church, St Andrew's, is a fine building rising up above a maze of picturesque cottages. Nearby is the Church House Inn, one of a great many to possess such a name in Devon. It was originally built as a chantry in 1100 and remained under the direct influence of the church until 1950. Most

of the pub buildings date back to the thirteenth century, a claim that is echoed in information given on the pub's sign.

Throughout all those years changes have occurred to the fabric of the building, some minor, others more dramatic. On one of those occasions ceiling plaster was removed to reveal the fluted timbers that once belonged to a room where monks used to gather for their meetings. It is in this part of the building where one solitary ghostlike monk is occasionally seen. It would seem that he must have been accustomed to attending many meetings there and cannot, therefore, kick the habit! The monk, if you see him, will probably be wearing a white habit and, if what witnesses say is correct, carrying a bucket!

CHURCH HOUSE INN, TORBRYAN

Torbryan is a small settlement not far from Ipplepen, set in a valley with limestone caves nearby. The countryside all around is Devon at its best with rolling green hills and narrow, twisting country lanes that take forever to get nowhere in particular. However, it's reckoned that at one time Torbryan was on an important stage coach route.

Set in this great countryside, wedged between Dartmoor and the sea, is a number of old cottages, a beautiful church (Holy Trinity) and, of course, the pub.

The ancient pub has its ghosts, of the variety that some folk can see quite clearly, whilst others see nothing at all. A classic example of this featured a local policeman, many years ago, who was new to the district and trying to acquaint himself with members of the local populace. He had gone into the pub, purely on community policing-type work, when he asked the landlord about the strange character ensconced in the corner, only to be told, in no uncertain terms, that there was nobody there!

The pub has its unaccountable footsteps and, because of its ecclesiastical background, its ghostly monks. A mid-nineteenth century landlord was reported to have seen them on several occasions but, apparently, wasn't too bothered by them. After all they make pretty quiet house guests, not being noted for their rowdiness.

The ghostly footsteps have had their active periods as well as their quiet times of inactivity. In 1963 the Bassett family took over the running of the inn. Within a month the footsteps were back, making positive strides to a bathroom. Several times David Bassett followed them only for them to fade away in its vicinity. Various theories were put forward, some just the products of over-imaginative minds. However, there was a general consensus of opinion that the person involved was a king, a monk, a farmer or a sailor. The latter was suggested as there was a school of thought that believed the oak panelling, which came from the church, previously originated from the cabin of an old sailing ship. In Victorian times a fierce fire destroyed the thatched roof of the pub and charred all the lintels, the ghost making less appearances in this era. It is thought that the

8

fire-shy ghost had suffered a violent death. Again there were various theories put forward by locals, which included death on the gallows on the nearby highway or murder at a hotly-contested cockfight. We shall probably never know but the four potential phantoms are all so different that it shouldn't be too difficult to identify which spook is which should you ever see one!

The pub is a popular one but its survival, as it is now, was under threat in 1937. There were plans to demolish this inn to replace it with a more functional modern one. Thank goodness they didn't for the ghostly footsteps would have had even more good reason to go on its regular romps for no self-respecting spook likes their cosy environment altered.

It has been estimated that there are about fifty pubs called the Church House Inn, most, of which, are in Devon. They were often built as dwellings to house stone masons, and other journeying tradesmen whilst churches were being built. In later times they were communal houses used for the sorts of activities that some members of the church did not wish to see taking place within God's House ... we are referring mostly to the consumption of alcohol!

COACH AND HORSES, BUCKLAND BREWER

This is a pub that David Young featured in his television series, and also in his book *More Cobblestones, Cottages and Castles*. He knows a good pub and a good story when he sees one and this pub, in this North Devon hilltop village, not surprisingly is full of history and full of ghosts.

The roof of this thirteenth century inn has been described as hedgehog-thatched, but beneath its cosy covering there have been some fairly strange goings-on. Although the road that passes through the village today is not an important routeway, in relative terms, in the past it was on a main coaching route, hence the pub's name. All manner of traveller visited the pub but it's one of those who did his gruesome and grisly work there that sends a shiver down the spine. Many people in Devon and Somerset have traced their family tree back only to find that one of their ancestors fell foul of the merciless, cold-hearted, ruthless Judge Jeffreys. The notorious judge travelled extensively in this area and it has been said that he held court in this pub.

The romantic yarn continues that those who were found guilty didn't have to wait long or, indeed, travel very far, to pay their debt to society. They were escorted up a narrow flight of steps to what was the hanging room. Here their wrists were strapped to the ceiling. A trap door beneath them, on which they were placed, was suddenly opened sending them plummeting down into the 'courtroom' below.

Various landlords have heard footsteps treading deliberately along above the oak beams when they have known that there has been nobody  upstairs. However, there is no evidence to substantiate the Judge Jeffreys connection with the pub and the present landlord, Ken Wolfe, has discovered that the notorious judge did not come as far west as Buckland Brewer.

One previous landlady reported to customers, and anyone who was prepared to listen, that she saw two cavaliers standing in the corner of the inn, close to where the trap door used to be. Unafraid of the spirits, she walked towards them with the intention of shaking their hands. However, these seventeenth century spooks were obviously antisocial creatures and, somewhat impolitely, simply faded away before she reached them. North Devon was the scene of several key battles and many other smaller scale skirmishes were witnessed in the Buckland Brewer area.

At Christmas-time, in 1978, some friends of the pub's owners were staying for a few days. One of these guests was awakened by a presence in the bedroom. This time the person **was** afraid, particularly as the shadowy figure approached her. The Civil War ghostly theme was continued but this time it was a Roundhead! As her fear grew the soldier disappeared and there were no further sightings for the couple.

The most recent apparitions have been of an entirely different nature. Late at night Ken Wolfe was certain that the lady who crossed a corridor was his daughter-in-law. However, when she was tackled about it the next day she was equally adamant that it was not her. On another occasion a regular saw who he thought was the landlady, Sue, cross the room and thought it very strange that she ignored him. It later transpired that Sue wasn't in the pub at the time.

The one fact common to these sightings was that the ghostly lady was in black, a fact that a previous landlord confirmed because he, too, had seen 'the Black Lady' on various occasions as well.

COOMBE CELLARS, COOMBEINTEIGNHEAD

This pub is sited on the south bank of the Teign Estuary and it was here, in 1968 where a young barmaid had a most alarming experience. Margaret Marshall, who lived-in, suddenly awoke feeling as if she were being strangled. Naturally she was petrified. She could not see or hear anyone but felt a definite presence. This sensation re-occurred and she was convinced that this room was haunted. She resorted to sleeping pills to help her sleep to help her through some difficult nights. But, as is often the case, despite telling everyone of her ordeal nobody took too much notice until...

The landlord went to a sale of paintings at the nearby market town of Newton Abbot and bought a batch of pictures. When he got home and had a closer look at his new acquisitions he had something of a shock. One of them was a macabre Victorian scene of a young lady being strangled. An even closer study of the picture revealed that the scene of this murder, in progress, was in the same room as Margaret Marshall's! Needless to say she moved to another one and it's believed there were no more disturbed nights for this young lady.

Others have experienced unpleasant feelings in the vicinity of this room. A man who

Haunted Pubs in Devon

had the job of installing an aerial in the attic, immediately above this room, was scared out of his wits but, although rendered a quaking wreck, with an ashen face, he refused to reveal what had triggered his terror.

COWICK BARTON, EXETER

Many buildings change their functions over the years. This pub, not far from the ever-spreading Marsh Barton Trading Estate in Exeter, is a good example, becoming a pub in 1963. At least one of its ghosts is a refugee from one of its previous uses, as a monastic cell. It's very much a case of 'old habits dying hard' for a benign old monk does, in his afterlife, what he did when he was alive. He looks after the sick so that when anyone has stayed there and not felt too well he's appeared to them, gazing concernedly over them as they lie in a state of semi-slumber. People who have experienced this unusual form of health care have commented how reassuring his expression has been. Nobody, to our knowledge, has been scared by him.

The pub is an ancient building that boasts another gentle ghost in the form of an old cavalier who shares the same interest in peoples' health, just like the monk. Could they be the same ghost in different guises? More details are given in our book *The Ghosts of Exeter*.

DARTMOOR INN, LYDFORD

"Hello, Good Evening and Welcome" was a well-known yesteryear catchphrase. It could, so easily, have been used by the ghost of this pub that has stood on the Okehampton-Tavistock road for several centuries. It was much used by packhorse drivers and seafarers heading for Plymouth in the past. It's said that every time a new landlord is installed a ghost appears to him, or her, in the first two weeks of their time there. Occasionally the ghost has been known to be mischievous, turning off the water supply or tampering with other items. Fortunately this ghostly activity, that has lasted several generations, has been normally on a temporary basis. Its boredom threshold seemed to be very low and it preferred to go into hibernation until the arrival of the next incumbent

However, in more recent years the spirit has been less shy and more forthcoming. On one occasion, when the bar was busy, in full view of those present, a beer glass rose into the air and headed off down the bar. Whilst regulars watched in amazement, another beer glass lifted itself off its hook and proceeded to follow it. The landlady had the presence of mind to notice a third one shaking on its hook, about to follow suit, so grabbed it quickly. The first two beer glasses suddenly fell to the ground, smashing on the bar floor.

Dartmoor letterbox enthusiasts may like to know that the pub has its own attractive letterbox stamp, available on request, to add to their collection.

EAST DART HOTEL, POSTBRIDGE

These days temperance hotels, that is those that do not retail alcohol, are few and far between. They were usually run by people with a strong religious conviction. This inn, at Postbridge, suddenly became 'converted' to a dry pub when the landlord's wife heard a passionate 'fire and brimstone' sermon about the 'Demon drink'. Immediately, she scurried home and, after talking to her husband, the inn ceased selling intoxicating substances. According to some sources this meant getting rid of all the alcohol by pouring it into a ditch on the opposite side of the road. What a waste!

The ghost is related to this saga as it's the ghost of a dog that visits the ditch to lap up the discarded drink. Nicely topped up, the dog climbs or staggers up the steep Merripit Hill, which rises from Postbridge towards Moreton, and begins to howl out at the moon. So, one dark night if, when driving over the moor, you see, looming out of the mist, a dog crooning at the moon, and seen in silhouette, you will know that this spectral canine critter is obviously well over the legal limit. The same hill is also haunted by some ghost pigs, but you'll have to read *Dark & Dastardly Dartmoor* to hear their story, as we won't 'squeal' on them here!

FISHERMAN'S COT, BICKLEIGH

This 1930s pub has an idyllic setting on the west bank of the River Exe by Bickleigh Bridge, where it has been rumoured that Paul Simon got his inspiration for his 'Bridge Over Troubled Water' song. It's known that his partner, Art Garfunkel, stayed there for we know a young lady who danced with him when he stayed here with his brother, before heading up to Scotland.

But did Mr Garfunkel ever meet the ghost that was around at that time?

Darren Yates had the job of locking up the bar every night after all the customers and the rest of the staff had gone home. On a number of occasions he was taken aback when the silence of an empty bar was punctuated by the laughter of a young lady in high spirits (no pun intended!).

Despite looking all around there was no sign of this young lady who had the habit of removing bottle tops from soft drinks and hurling them around the bar. Darren's pair of chocolate-coloured Labradors always reacted to the visitations, either by crouching down in fear behind the bar or leaping over it in their haste to get out of the building. The ghostly giggling hasn't been heard that often in recent times.

We've all heard some of the weird excuses to appear on insurance claim forms, like "I was driving along the road and hit a lamppost that wasn't there" so it makes you wonder what sort of excuses just might be thrown up by a startled motorist navigating the bridge on a June night – a Midsummer Night's Nightmare perhaps…

In late June 1981 the *Express & Echo*, Exeter and East Devon's evening newspaper, carried the following story:

"Suddenly, though, there it was … the unmistakable clip-clop of hooves and the shadowy headless rider, in armour, at the end of the village's 400-year-old bridge.

Nineteen year old Joanna Cruwys, of Exeter, was hoping for a glimpse of the ghost of the man her ancestor slew on the bridge in 1332.

He was Sir Alexander Cruwys who ran through a member of Bickleigh's Carew family with his sword and then threw the body into the downstream side of the Exe.

Ever since that fateful day – so the Bickleigh legend goes – he rides across Bickleigh Bridge on June 24.

Last night saw the first, official, Bickleigh ghost watch. Mr Meredith, a county council official in Exeter, organised it all right down to a couple of British Railway red and green signalling lamps to stop the traffic on the night.

Right on time the rider rode ... but the horse turned out to be a pony that made straight for Happy Meadow, the village cricket ground, and the man on horseback suddenly dismounted and the armour-bearer made his way towards Bickleigh Castle. "

The article did not say who the man was but the impression is that someone tried to pull a fast one. Fortunately no road accidents, as yet, have occurred as a result of startling spectral ghost appearances on Bickleigh Bridge.

In some ways it is a shame that someone tried to imitate Sir Alexander as two hundred eager-to-be-spooked spectators had assembled in the garden of The Fisherman's Cot, as it was a fine vantage point. The pub put on refreshments and was a scene of great revelry and high expectation as the time drew towards the anticipated spectral happening. But there was also confusion over the timing of the ghostly guest appearance for would it be midnight or 1.00 a.m. (was the knight in BST or GMT?) And would any self-respecting spook appear to such a throng? Those who claim to have seen him on other occasions provide the details that Sir Alexander is much shorter as a ghost than he was when mortal. This is because, as a ghost, he crosses the bridge with his head tucked under his left arm (something like a rugby player in a scrum), and wields a sword in his right hand. His attack on a Carew was, apparently, the result of an argument about a fair lady. What is particularly strange about the choice of venue for this ghostly apparition, dating back to 1332, is that this particular bridge wasn't there in his time! Normally such ghosts follow the alignment of previous structures, which is why sometimes they appear half-submerged in the ground whilst at other times they are high off the ground. Their surroundings have changed but they find it difficult to break the habits of a lifetime.

Sir Alexander's spirit is not the only one here for several haunt the bridge and its environs. Another, this time a lady, is sometimes seen walking across the river beneath the bridge, just above the weir. This is an experience that locals can only match in times of severe drought when the river runs at a trickle. There were pictures in the press, in September 1933, when locals were photographed in mid stream. In January 1940 the river partly froze over here but nobody was foolhardy enough to test the thickness of the ice.

THE GEORGE, HATHERLEIGH

If you read the sign on the wall you will see that here, when it comes to eating, you are in the company of 'royalty' and rich food but whether this is wishful thinking or not you will have to find out for yourself.

This hostelry is an ancient one dating back to the fourteenth century so it's had centuries to cultivate its ghosts. In The George's years of trading thousands of stage coaches must have trundled past its doors and, if some folk are to be believed, still do! A phantom coach has been heard approaching the inn but no reason has been given for its visit.

Within the inn there have been various ghosts. One guest felt such a cold rush of air that they were absolutely convinced that somebody had opened a window but an inspection revealed no suitable apertures for this internal breeze. On opening the door he was confronted with the apparition of a transparent woman, shrouded in a halo of light, drifting along the corridor. Apparently there is no suggestion of who the ghost is or why she emits such a freezing cold mass of air as she passes through this fine old hotel. Is she the Queen that is mentioned on the sign outside? We think not as she promises a warm reception!

THE GLOBE INN, BRIXHAM

This was just one of a number of stories that former Brixham resident, Graham Wyley, collected for his entertaining book *The Ghosts of Brixham*. Graham has an uncanny ability to seek out ghosts and, if needs be, sort them out, indeed, in recent years he has become a leading authority on such matters.

In this story you must consider the various strange goings-on at the Globe Inn, built about 1790 and located in Fore Street, and see for yourself if there's anything in it. It's a building that used to advertise itself as 'the oldest commercial hotel in the town with good stabling.'

A previous landlord, in the mid-1980s, was taken ill and found himself recuperating at a convalescent home in Newton Abbot. In the course of conversations with fellow patients he discovered that one little old lady patient had been born, about the turn of the century, at the Globe Inn. Her mother had worked there in the days when labour saving devices were called servants.

She was naturally inquisitive about the state of the pub but her first question helped to raise the recuperating landlord's blood pressure. "How's the ghost? Is he still wandering up and down the stairs?" The landlord had, indeed, experienced various nocturnal knockings. He and his wife had been woken a number of times by the most uncanny sounds all round their bed of hobnail boots on bare floorboards. This was particularly baffling for the room was carpeted!

The landlord's daughters came down to visit their parents at the pub and were given a bedroom to share. Their first night was eventful with a curtain being moved to and fro all night long. This so unnerved them that they refused, point blank, to sleep in that room again.

Another episode, with which they found hard to come to terms, involved the annual visit of the crew of HMS *Palister* to the area. On such occasions the crew stayed for a few nights at the Globe. After one visit the visitors' book went missing and a bit of skylarking was suspected, it being felt that one of the more boisterous crew members had taken it in fun, perhaps to post it back later from some distant clime.

The year went its full cycle and the landlord had long-forgotten the missing book. However, on the very day that the vessel was scheduled to return to Brixham the missing book appeared, as if by magic, lying behind the bar, in full view, and covered in a year's worth of dust.

But landlords, like the vessels in Brixham's harbour, come and go, and new tenants arrived to make the Globe their 'Brave New World.' The locals were full of it, having heard a catalogue of ghost stories from various tenants over the years. After all there was good mileage to be had in the lively bar room banter. If they could send a new landlord and landlady to bed with such spooky stories ringing in their ears it would certainly make them sit up with a start if there were any sudden noises in the night!

But the locals had to bide their time for the ghost of the Globe was in no hurry to upset the new incumbents. Three months had elapsed before anything remotely unusual occurred. The first incident bore similarities to the saga of the visitors' book. A piece of embroidery, belonging to an aunt, had been stowed away in a box. However, the very day before the aunt was due to arrive, the piece of embroidery, if you'll excuse the pun, suddenly materialised on the lounge floor.

All the signs point to it probably being a female ghost, and there is no intention to be sexist here, as the items that have been tampered with are ladies' possessions such as jewellery, ladies underclothes and so on. Despite the frequent nocturnal removing of various items they have, for the most part, turned up within days but in completely different locations from where they had originally been.

Graham Wyley observed that it was as if, whenever new tenants arrived, there was a recharging of the spirit's strength and power. Perhaps, too, there may be an element that ghosts, like mortals, get bored and welcome a fresh challenge, something we have already seen at the Dartmoor Inn.

This ghost, whoever he or she may be, has a bit of an edge to its personality for whenever anyone has had the gall to question its very existence, it has taken up the challenge to prove their doubts were unfounded. Various visitors have learnt that to scoff is a foolhardy thing to do and instead of having the proverbial 'egg on their faces' have, at least, had their beer poured over them by an invisible presence – now doesn't that sound more like a woman!

GLOBE INN, CHAGFORD

Old postcard views of this inn invariably show stage coaches outside, ready for the off, probably to Exeter, a journey guaranteed to rattle the bones if ever there was one. Its ghost is a reflection of the quality of justice that existed in the days of witch hunts, when any persons remotely thought to be associated with such practices were 'tested' to see if they were one or not. The problem was that the 'test' often involved immersing the victim in water. If the person drowned she wasn't a witch! If she didn't it was off to the stake and a fatal appointment with an old flame. We tell

you all this as background information to this pub's ghost, a seventeenth century chambermaid, as she was proven not to be a witch and drowned in the test. This was obviously small compensation for her as her troubled spirit sometimes is felt in the Azalea Room.

Globe Inn is a common name for a pub and it's believed that many that bore this name, in times past, did so as an indication that they sold Portuguese wines.

THE INN ON THE GREEN, PAIGNTON

Paignton's sea front green is its pride and joy. It's an open space reclaimed from coastal marshes and a fine place for recreational activities like ball games or for throwing Frisbees and other playful projectiles. It's also an ideal venue, fanned by a gentle sea breeze, on a fine, sunny, Paignton morning for the more passive leisure activity of lying in a recumbent, blissful semi-comatose posture, ensconced in a deck chair. But while the visitors lie there contentedly snoozing, just across the Green are some other sleeping spirits…

The Inn on the Green originally bore the less trendy name of The Prince Regent. It also used to have a tower, visible in old picture postcard views, where 'Alfred' used to haunt the guests, but this was pulled down. However, Alfred has shown himself to be undaunted by this displacement and has relocated himself into a cellar where there are beer barrels. Apparently he plays with any switches or taps that take his fancy, quite possibly causing mischief to repay, in his own mind, those who evicted him from his previous abode in the tower. Deryck Seymour has included more details in his *Ghosts of Torbay*.

KING'S ARMS, BUCKFASTLEIGH

Do you remember when the crowds thronged to Buckfastleigh Races? You don't? Well if you have travelled the great highway that links Exeter to Plymouth, and other points west, you will have surely noticed the grandstand, about a mile from Buckfastleigh, that stands looking so forlorn in the middle of a field. Itself it looks like a ghost and if it could talk it could tell enough tales to give Dick Francis many more good racing yarns. The King's Arms' past is inextricably linked with the old racecourse for it was here that the race headquarters were set up.

The pub is several centuries old and is an old coaching inn but its ghost does not have any equine connections, as far as we know. The ghost has a limited wardrobe that extends to a simple long grey dress. In it she is often seen at the bottom of a staircase in a hallway. Her story is a tragic one for there she was, biding her time at the inn, waiting for her loved one to arrive, when she had the great misfortune to fall down the well that was there in those days.

KING'S ARMS HOTEL, KINGSBRIDGE

The lower part of Kingsbridge's main street is very steep so the ghost that haunts this hotel has wisely opted to choose the part of the thoroughfare that won't render her too breathless.

Having been a blushing bride in 1798, when this was a relatively new establishment (founded 1775) she must have been excited at the prospect of the honeymoon night. Alas something must have gone terribly wrong for the 'intended' did a runner and was never seen again. We can only conjecture that what he thought he was going to get failed to reach his expectations or, quite simply, that he wasn't ready for the joys of marital bliss.

The poor girl was obviously so upset by this that in death, and we don't know how many years elapsed before this event, her troubled soul returns to the scene of her great trauma to haunt the honeymoon hotel.

KINGSBRIDGE INN, TOTNES

The Good Town of Totnes is a very old one and it possesses so many ghosts that we recommend *The Ghosts of Totnes* by Bob Mann, which deals with most of them. However, for this publication we are only concerned with those haunted buildings that are pubs so hope we are not giving too many secrets away from that entertaining and informative book. So as not to impinge on Bob Mann's excellent book, we have left out some of his other haunted inns from this South Devon town.

The Kingsbridge Inn is in Leechwell Street at the top end of the town and, as you may have guessed, on the original road to Kingsbridge. The pub has several ghosts and there have been many apparitions to customers and staff throughout the years. But by virtue of being a pub it has its 'regulars'. Mary Brown is one of them, having been a barmaid here in the seventeenth century. She was the unfortunate victim of an evil landlord who seduced her, murdered her and concealed her body within the walls of the building ... or so the story goes. It could well have an element of truth because Mary only reveals herself to other women. This was the case in the early 1970s when the landlord's daughter took days to get over the shock! Many other ladies have seen Mary since.

There used to be the favourite chair of a previous landlady kept in the pump room. Long after she had passed away she was spotted, several times, sitting in it.

THE KING'S HEAD, CULLOMPTON

The widest part of Cullompton's main street is called The Bull Ring and in and around it are a number of old pubs where travellers could seek refreshment on their journeys through the English countryside. Today similar needs are often satisfied by motorway service stations. Cullompton's pubs struggle on and, despite the loss of much of the passing trade, offer other delights, such as ghosts. Four of the town's pubs are featured, thus making it the unofficial capital for haunted hotels and pubs in Devon, at least in terms of a ratio of ghosts to the number of licensed premises.

This pub is named after Charles II who, unlike his father, Charles I, managed to keep his head. It's there to see on the pub sign! Despite the history lesson, the ghost is not from that period of history nor is he English. It's believed that an American airman was involved in a violent confrontation in the public bar and was fatally stabbed. Troubled by his untimely death, he has been back to haunt the pub.

THE LEWTRENCHARD HOTEL, LEWTRENCHARD

Lewtrenchard is a beautiful parish not far from the northwestern edge of Dartmoor. Its hotel takes its name from it, a beautiful establishment that has been featured a number of times on television, for it was the home of the celebrated Rev. Sabine Baring-Gould, prolific author and traveller, a man of great energy and talent who died in 1924.

The hotel is haunted by Madam Gould, a rarity amongst ghosts for she was a lady of great strength when alive and almost equally as purposeful when dead.

Madam Gould refused to go to her deathbed on 10 April 1795. She just sat in a chair as she finally drifted off into the next world. Almost immediately the window shutters were flung open and within an hour of her death her ghost was appearing to people in the house. Whilst her body had been laid out on a bed upstairs, a servant girl gazed from this room to see Madam Gould stood beneath a walnut tree in the grounds.

A week later a man named Symonds thought nothing of seeing her in a field by the River Lew. Madam was sat on a plough and waved to Symonds. The reason for his calmness stemmed from the fact that he had just returned from America and wasn't aware that she was dead!

Many people saw her after that. She appeared to people walking on Galford Down, not far away. There were occasional sightings but nothing quite as dramatic as the events that occurred on a dull day in 1832...

A carpenter, who was working in the church, had heard of Madam Gould's spiritual sauntering, so decided to peer inside her vault. Madam Gould

was not amused! She showed her immense displeasure at the intrusion by rising out of her grave to chase the startled carpenter out of the church, across a field all the way to his home. He didn't have to look behind for her ghost gave out such a light that it cast a shadow over him as he fled homewards. A little more than thirty years later another man believed that he had encountered Madam's ghost near a mine shaft. In trying to get away he tripped and broke a leg.

One of Madam Gould's regular visitors to Lewtrenchard House, now a hotel, was Parson Elford. Both have been spied since their deaths sat together in the drawing room. There have been many other sightings of this good lady. She was particularly fond of children so that on some occasions, when children staying at the hotel have felt unwell, Madam Gould has appeared to see how they are and to make sure they are being cared for. She appears as a smiling old lady, usually in a dark coloured dress.

MANOR HOUSE HOTEL, CULLOMPTON

Can you picture Miss Haversham from Charles Dickens' *Great Expectations*? This poor lady was left abandoned at the altar on her wedding day and never slipped out of her wedding dress, into something more comfortable, staying in it for many years. The closest that you will get to it in the ghost world, apart from at the Kingsbridge Inn, is in this hotel where a young lady in a wedding dress, also jilted on her wedding day, supposedly haunts room 6. She may also be there for this might well have been her honeymoon room or she may come from the days of yesteryear when this was a private residence.

Within the same group of buildings there are other ghosts. One of them is a most unhappy soldier who deserted his comrades but was soon caught and subsequently shot.

MANOR INN, ASHWATER

The small village of Ashwater, with a population of about 600, is almost as far west as you can go in Devon before reaching Cornwall. It lies just a few miles inside the border and is about half way between Holsworthy and Launceston. It's not far from the even more westerly hamlet of Luffincott, a remote retreat that yielded a most bizarre story for *Ghastly and Ghostly Devon*.

The village of Ashwater clusters around its attractive triangular green, a much quieter place than perhaps it may have been when its pub used to be the hunting lodge. The walls still possess pictures of hunting scenes and it could be that the pub's resident ghost is a by-product of these former activities. Where the bar is today used to be where the great gun racks once stood. The upstairs was reserved for servants' quarters. There are two fireplaces, the unhappy ghost of the pub, possibly a victim of some tragic accident, occasionally appears out of the burning embers of one of them. Another theory, again with no proven truth, was that this was a man who was opposed to the railway that came through this neighbourhood in the late nineteenth century and so perturbed was he, that he topped himself. If he could have lived long enough he could have seen it both come and go again, its departure making the village that bit more remote than it already was.

MONK'S RETREAT, BROADHEMPSTON

You will just have to take our word for this next story! It was just prior to the publication of Deryck Seymour's *A Secret Circle*, a little book about all the villages in the vicinity of Broadhempston, when we paid a visit to this inn.

Sat in this pub we chatted with the landlady, but whilst we talked I (Chips) sniffed for there was a strong and distinct smell wafting up that I recognised from my childhood. (This had been spent at a convent school in Exeter, which I attended until I was about seven.) The unmistakable smell was of incense. But nobody else could smell it at all, not even the slightest whiff. Now if truth be told my nose is a bit of a whopper but when it comes to savouring smells it's not the most sensitive organ in the universe and I'm usually the last person to detect even the most pungent of smells. *A Secret Circle* was published a few days later and we were stunned to see reference, in almost a throw away line, to the occasional, inexplicable smell of incense. It stated that this was most common at Easter, or on other religiously significant dates, but as far as we were aware, this was just a plain old pagan sort of day.

The ghost is naturally of a monk and one that has done his bit for the preservation of the pub. A lit candle threatened to be the cause of a fire as nobody noticed it catch a table alight. Fortunately the ghostly monk came out of the shadows, rapped on the table (not in the modern musical style but in the fist punching fashion!) and drew attention to the blaze. As the throng rushed to deal with it the 'monk's retreat' into the shadows, from whence he came, was a silent one.

THE NEW INN, COLEFORD

You can almost bet your bottom dollar that any building or street with 'New' in the name is exceedingly old! This thatched inn, not many miles from Crediton, is no different and dates back to the thirteenth century. You would also stand a good chance, in any wager, that any New Inn, wherever it may be, would be haunted. After all such buildings have had ample time to witness untimely deaths, tragedies or simply just the weight of numbers passing through them. People who lived in the past stood far more chance of becoming ghosts than people of today, or so statistics would seem to suggest, perhaps as there was more misery then.

This New Inn's ghost has the grand name of 'Sebastian' and other than he is a monk who occasionally roams the ancient inn, little is known of him or his circumstances.

THE NORTHMORE ARMS, WONSON

Where's Wonson you all ask? If you had to name the one pub that was difficult to find, in this book, then this would be the one! Your best bet is to locate Throwleigh and then ask for directions. Do you recall that we mentioned, when looking at the Bay Horse at Ashburton,

the sailors or mariners that walked across Devon to pick up new ships when they went from ports at either of the county? You do? Good! This tiny inn is also on that route known as The Mariners' Way and its ghost is, appropriately, that of a sailor, complete with a beautiful set of old-fashioned mutton-chop sailorly whiskers. This is without even the hint of the smell of the salt spray on the wind at a pub that's almost as far away from the sea as one could be in Devon. He must have been one of those leg-weary travellers who didn't quite make it, this being his last 'port of call'. If you see someone there who looks a bit like 'Captain Bird's Eye' then this your man!

THE OLD INN, WIDECOMBE

In sharp contrast to the last town, everyone knows Widecombe! The famous folk song has put this tiny moorland village well and truly on the map and in the season thousands flock there to see for themselves what all the fuss was about. The Old Inn is right in the centre of the village, surrounded by thriving gift shops.

The inn has expanded over the years to accommodate the constant invasion of visitors and despite a major fire in 1977 now boasts several bars. Old "Harry" has plenty of space to fill in his ghostly wanderings, ones that he has done ever since he was murdered! Mid-afternoon is his spiritual stalking time, his favoured route being from the kitchen into a room that has no exit. He doesn't alarm those who see him for he is as solid as they are and until he walks through the wall they don't realise that he's a ghost!

There is also a weeping girl, yet another, who sobs for hours until the door of the room that she is in opens and peace reigns again.

PALACE HOTEL, TORQUAY

There is no way, really, that you should lump this magnificent hotel with some of the more modest establishments also featured here but as it has a ghost, it's been included. The name Palace, in this instance, originates from a bishop's residence. It was here, in a much smaller house, now absorbed into the luxury hotel, that Henry Phillpotts, Bishop of Exeter, had his home. He was a man who knew his own mind, and, if rumours are to be believed, that of others as well. He was so strong-willed that, even in death, he continues to influence people with his frequent ghostly appearances. He has appeared to guests, porters and chambermaids. One specific sighting was by a deputy head porter, Mr Mitchell. On 8 November 1978 Bishop Phillpotts appeared right in front of him but appeared to Mr Mitchell as if he were stood behind a lace curtain. Out of curiosity he immediately walked towards the Bishop, who was fully attired in his Victorian bishop's dress, but as he did so the ghost faded away leaving only a wedge of cold air in its wake. He might be mystified, and no doubt quite miffed as to why his retirement home is constantly so full of people.

THE PIG AND WHISTLE, LITTLEHEMPSTON

This pub lies on the main road from Totnes to Newton Abbot, its ghost being well-known for a number of years as it has cropped up in most books of the supernatural kind. The pub is not far from the most haunted castle in England, Berry Pomeroy, where you can discover, in Deryck Seymour's *Ghosts of Berry Pomeroy Castle*, a whole variety of amazing ghostly tales whilst learning something of the history of this eminent pile of ruins.

Here, though, we have come to meet Freddie, a ghostly womanising monk. It transpires that far from being celibate, this amorous monk would ride miles from the abbey, possibly Buckfast, to meet his secret love at the inn, a lady of easy virtue.

Whenever anyone from the abbey came remotely near he was supposed to beat a hasty retreat, via an underground passage, to a nearby chapel. Safely in the sanctuary of this place of worship, he would get out his beads and start praying fervently. It looks as if he needed to do this for his ghostly form feels guilty enough to return to the pub. He still uses the same entrance, even though it has been blocked up and turned into a window. People sitting in the bar, throughout the years, have been taken by surprise to see this former door, now a window, open and close without any apparent help. We wonder how frustrated the monk gets when he finds his true love not there to greet him … or is she? If you ever see the monk, have a close look to see if there's a smile on his face!

THE PILCHARD INN, BURGH ISLAND, BIGBURY-ON-SEA

Bright and breezy Burgh Island is the place to be on 13 August each year if you want to join the ghost of Tom Crocker. Until 1939 people used to make an annual pilgrimage to the island, dressed in pirates' or smugglers' costumes, to keep him company for this was the day that he was apparently shot dead outside the Pilchard Inn and the one, of several, when he returned to his old haunt.

He was an out and out rascal who got his inevitable comeuppance but he refuses to remain at rest. From time to time he appears on other occasions. At the entrance to the pub there are a pair of heavy double doors, like those found in stables. Sometimes, even on very calm days, these will rattle or bang shut with a great force and, apparently, there is never anyone around when it happens!

"Lovejoy", the popular television series of the 1980s and 90s, was based in the counties of Norfolk and Suffolk but in each series there was at least one episode that featured an area outside the series' homeland. And, sure enough, the roguish antique dealer, played by Ian McShane, no stranger to the county, visited the hotel on Burgh Island and filmed in the tiny Pilchard Inn. In the episode, where he retrieved a hidden treasure from behind a cavity in the wall, he also referred to this ghost – so it must be real!

To get to the island when the tide is in it's necessary to cross the submerged sand bar using an unusual sea-tractor. One of its former pilots, who gave years of sterling service, was the late, heavily-bewhiskered Jimbo Brenton. He was scared out of his wits on a number of occasions by old Tom Crocker, but he did like an occasional drink or three ... More about this unusual island and the surrounding coastline can be discovered in *Burgh Island and Bigbury Bay*, dedicated specifically to the area in and around the island.

PRINCE OF WALES, PRINCETOWN

If you were a ghost, the last place you'd want to haunt would be draughty old Princetown, England's highest and probably most windswept town. If a ghost is as light as air, any ghost stepping out of the shelter of home here will, no doubt, be blown miles. However there are some redeeming features in this Dartmoor settlement for there are some pleasant pubs. The oldest, the Plume of Feathers, has its ghosts that are featured in *Dark and Dastardly Dartmoor*. To our knowledge another inn – The Devil's Elbow – seems strangely devoid of spooks. This leaves us with the Prince of Wales, suitably named in honour of a previous Prince of Wales. Its ghost is a priest, a harmless man of God, who is a bit of a drifter for that is how he propels himself through the air, but is this anything to do with the wind that seems to howl through keyholes?

PROSPECT INN, EXETER

This pub, on Exeter Quay, may give you the feeling of déjà-vû as you enter it for the first time, as it was used for the filming of the BBC's *The Onedin Line* so if you have seen any of the episodes, the interior may be familiar. But it's not the ghosts of old sea-dogs or agitated film directors, luvvie, that haunt this pub. It's unlikely that any customers will ever see the little girl who haunts The Prospect because she only appears in an upper room and only at Christmas. Nobody seems to know who she is other than she is in Victorian costume and clutches a soft toy, probably a doll. She has a radiant smile but doesn't linger, fading away within seconds of being seen.

Had you been around in the mid 1950s you could have had the opportunity of winning this pub as it was a prize in the *Daily Sketch* newspaper. The late, blonde bombshell, Diana Dors, presented it to the winner. However, it has not always been a happy pub as one landlord committed suicide by hanging himself. He has not returned ... yet.

THE RING O'BELLS, CHAGFORD

The ghosts here are not up to much, simply banging, sometimes noisily, away in an empty cellar and occasionally tossing pictures off the wall. It is considered to be a case of the upheaval of rewiring and installing new plumbing that has disturbed some of the spirits that have previously slumbered here. The Crowner, a variant of Coroner, was a visitor to the pub in the past, not for refreshment but to preside over inquests over those who died in unexpected or unusual circumstances. He had a long journey having to come all the way from Black Torrington.

ROCK INN, HAYTOR VALE

There seems to be no shortage of ghost stories where a heinous crime has led to some poor soul being condemned to troop the floorboards in their lonely night vigil. This

24

lovely inn in the lee of the moor, tucked below the great granite mass of Haytor Rock, gives us Belinda, a former serving wench at the inn.

Her fatal mistake was to embark on a passionate affair with a coachman who was already married. On finding out about the affair the coachman's wife was less than pleased about the situation. Her retribution was gained at the pub where she murdered the wench. History does not relate what she did to her husband! Belinda now wears grey and is not an idle spectre for she is seen, from time to time, sweeping the upstairs floors of the Rock Inn.

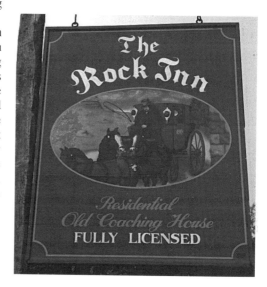

One resident, to whom the wee small hours had a literal meaning, left his room and on descending a staircase noticed a girl in a grey uniform cleaning the stairs. Too tired to question her presence, at such an 'unearthly' hour, he told the landlord, the following morning, that he pushed his staff too hard if they were working at two in the morning! The guest was then informed that staff at the Rock Inn wore black not grey, and work civilised hours. This was not a member of staff but, in all likelihood, a ghost!

In addition to 200+-year-old Belinda's extra curricular activities there have also been other strange and unaccountable nocturnal happenings. There are certain upstairs rooms where, for no logical reason, items of the electrical and plumbing type spring to life. Radios, lights, taps and flushes all start up with apparently nobody there to take the blame, much to the dismay of those occupying these rooms at the time. Even more dramatic was the incident when a guest reported strange noises overhead. There was nothing wrong with the structure of the ceiling, but the following night it collapsed onto the bed. Luckily there was nobody occupying it that night!

ROYAL CASTLE HOTEL, DARTMOUTH

Deryck Seymour's *The Ghosts of Torbay* has been the source of some of these stories and also this short one from Dartmouth. It involves a naughty ghost ...

This sixteenth century hotel occupies a prime position in Dartmouth overlooking not just the Boatfloat but also the shimmering waters of the Dart.

The hotel, and one room in particular, has had something of a reputation as a haunted one for years so a lady journalist decided to do a bit of ghost-hunting. Such spiritual safaris are often a complete waste of time as ghosts simply do not play to the gallery or appear on cue but this lady struck lucky, if that's the right phrase to use in this context. She had a night punctuated by disturbances of one kind or another. The culminating gesture was the discovery of her bra, which thus had been subjected to yet another 'uplifting' experience by having been slung across the room to be found by the priest's hole. Fortunately she was not wearing it at the time! Perhaps this is a salutary lesson for it was the ghost who did the ghost-'busting'!

Haunted Pubs in Devon

25

History suggests that this hotel was favoured by Charles II who used it as a venue to off-load his various mistresses. One of them who suffered this fate was never seen again! An early morning in November is another to note down in your own ghost-busting diary for it's on one of those cool mornings that another ghostly spectre looms large at this hotel. A coach and horses will be heard, but not seen, as if they are driving over cobblestones of which there are no longer any. It's believed that the coach was sent here to pick up Mary, consort of William III, in order to convey her to meet him at Torquay. Some have claimed that the noise is most audible from within the hotel for this is, supposedly, where the cobbles were before the inn was extended forwards. It's also believed that one hotel porter was so unnerved by the various hotel hauntings that he resigned because of them.

SHIP INN, EXETER

Most Ship Inns are situated in ports, coastal settlements or immediately beside rivers or canals but this one isn't! The Ship Inn is one of Exeter's most famous inns, and lies on a narrow lane between Exeter's High Street and the Cathedral Green. It's an ancient inn, one that boasts such famous visitors as Sir Francis Drake. It is believed that this was his "Favourite Port of Call" and that he planned and plotted the downfall of the Spanish Armada whilst quaffing his ale here. One story that has gone the rounds suggests that Drake quaffed so much ale at The Ship Inn that the landlord banned him from the inn unless he was accompanied by a more discerning drinker who would keep an eye on Drake's intake of ale and assume responsibility for the great man's behaviour.

Now the chances are that you will have never heard of Mrs Gill who lived and worked at the Ship Inn, not in the first Elizabethan epoch but the second. She was a cleaner there so worked either before the pub was open or after it had closed. When she was there the place was very quiet – enough to hear a pin drop. She had heard rumours that the pub was haunted but being an eminently sensible woman dismissed such stories as 'stuff and nonsense.' However, as she cleaned some of the upper rooms, she was aware that, occasionally, all wasn't quite normal and on the few occasions that this was the case she was pushed down a short flight of steps. The first time it bemused her, the second time it led to her seeking employment elsewhere! A disbelieving friend suffered a similar fate

Haunted Pubs in Devon

and also soon left the job. The suggestion is that the only person it could be is Sir Francis Drake, a man who must be as busy as a ghost as he was when he was alive for he haunts a host of ghost places.

SIR WALTER RALEIGH INN, EAST BUDLEIGH

This is one of a small number of pubs in East Devon to have been haunted. The pub lies in one of Devon's prettiest villages with all sorts of possibilities for walks with Woodbury Common's wide open spaces and a network of footpaths and quiet lanes all ideal for planning a route to include this pub.

Sir Walter Raleigh was born in a lovely country house called Hayes Barton, up one of these quiet thoroughfares, Hayes Lane. For the sake of the book it would have been more exciting to claim that this great man's ghost often walked in the inn with his head tucked under his arm, but this is not the case. His spirit is believed to have made occasional visits but the feelings and sensations have generally been rather low key. Perhaps you'll have better luck and see him in a more dramatic repose!

SMUGGLERS HAUNT, BRIXHAM

Brixham, as we have already seen, is a fishing town of narrow streets and back alleys or drangs. It is also of numerous steep stone steps, of quaint cottages with hidey holes and, in the past, of men who smuggled as a way of supplementing a meagre income.

The Smugglers Haunt is paradoxically not haunted by a smuggler! Instead a young girl who fell to her death from an upper room, when it was a cottage, is now one of the two resident ghosts. 'Aggie', as she is known, met with her fatal accident in about 1920. The room, from which she hurtled headlong to the unyielding street below, has been subject to various supernatural experiences. Guests have suddenly had the bedclothes pulled off them. Lights, that they have just switched on, have been suddenly switched off again. This ghost, though from the pre-television age, has also been known to switch on the television on many occasions.

The other resident ghost can best be envisaged by recalling how Dudley Moore looked when he teamed up with the now late Peter Cook in 'Not Only...But Also.' Here is a ghost with dark hair, probably about forty years old, with a cloth cap and a full length raincoat right down to his ankles. This ghost is a little taller than the diminutive comedian but is always seen at the same table, sometimes standing, at other times sitting. The hotel has obviously got some magnetism for spooks for there have been numerous inexplicable occurrences in other parts of the building but none of them are smugglers at the Smugglers Haunt. Perhaps after a life of evasion as mortals they are equally good in the hereafter!

STEAM PACKET, TOTNES

This pub, on the banks of the River Dart at Totnes, has one of the most pleasant locations of any of the pubs or hotels featured in this book. Its ghost is not very well

documented so not much can be said of it other than it's a friendly spirit that contents itself by putting on or turning off lights, and opening or closing doors, but not in any form of courtesy, just when it has a mind to be mischievous. It has showed its other practical side by turning off the water. The vibrations felt here are good ones. It's likely that the Dart, which flows beside it, with its reputation of luring people to a watery death, is more haunted and sinister than any of the pubs along its banks!

THATCHED INN, ABBOTSHAM

There have not been too many haunted pubs from the North Devon area included in this book but one that surfaced in *Tales of the Unexplained in Devon* is this old inn, which is haunted by a former taxi driver, at Abbotsham, just a short taxi drive from Bideford.

This pub was originally called the New Inn, changed its name to the Thatched House Inn, but since February 1993 it has been simply the Thatched Inn. Running any pub has always been a tough task and this one has had its up and downs. Henry Tucker, who was the landlord throughout the 1920s and 30s combined his pub duties with also being the local carrier. Another landlord, since the war, was also milkman, postman, driving instructor and chief bottlewasher!

The ghostly manifestations have included clinking glasses, which could indicate a couple sharing a ghostly drink. There have been the sounds of footsteps with no apparent body, or feet, to match them. Resident dogs have also reacted to the various presences that have been felt here.

There are precious few hard facts about the precise identity of who the person or persons might be in this ghostly toasting. One customer believed that the taxi driver was partial to a glass of Advocaat and when a glass of this was left in an upstairs room, overnight on his birthday, it was found to be empty the next day. The popular belief is that he was having an illicit affair and that his taxi, with him at the wheel, went over the cliffs in suspicious circumstances. This all happened many years ago but his ghostly tippling doesn't seem to bother anybody.

THREE CROWNS HOTEL, CHAGFORD

Without doubt this is one of the more famous of the places mentioned in this volume of ghost pubs in Devon. It has a long history and is given fuller treatment in *The Great Little Chagford Book*.

We wonder if any of the more famous visitors to the pub have seen any of its spooks, for many well known guests have graced its portal.

In the English Civil War a young Royalist, of high standing, called Sidney Godolphin, was wounded in a skirmish at Chagford and it's believed that he was carried to the porch of this ancient inn where he died. He was just thirty years old, a sensitive, highly intelligent man with many attributes. Rumours of his ghost have gone on ever since but it still took local man and one of the hotel's chefs, Jock Hardie, completely by surprise, when he came to face with Sidney in June 1980. He had been employed there for some ten years but had seen nothing until the ghostly Godolphin appeared, complete with large plumed hat and full cavalier dress, at the door to the dining room.

Other reports of Sidney suggest that he is, which may surprise some people, a rare phenomenon amongst ghosts for he often does the old, stereotyped party trick of walking through walls. The granite ones at the Three Crowns are so solid that only a ghost could go through them.

TORS HOTEL, BELSTONE

The hotel is situated in the sprawling northern Dartmoor village of Belstone, a few miles from Okehampton and beneath the great towering hill, that can be seen from almost anywhere in the county, known as Cosdon, by locals, and Cawsand Beacon by others.

The pub has had, and continues to host, ghosts at infrequent times. On one occasion when there were no guests staying, the landlord made his way up to bed, around midnight, and as he climbed the back stairs he felt an icy blast of cold air pass his face. That same night he was roused from his slumbers by a tap on his bedroom door (which, as any comedian will tell you, is a strange place for a tap!) His immediate reaction was that this was his young son but, in that half conscious state of an interrupted sleep, he discovered that his son was fast asleep and snugly settled in his bed.

But that wasn't all as, when he first took over the running of the pub, there were many instances, in his first few months there, when inexplicable cases of door-banging went on upstairs when he and others knew that there could be no mortals up there and no draughts to cause this to happen.

Needless to say the landlord made polite enquiries, to long-established locals, as to what they thought the knockings and rumblings might be. The consensus of opinion is that this was a landlady of yesteryear who died at the pub. The ghost is no problem as it generates a feeling of friendliness. Although she hasn't been seen, mysterious shadows in the hallway, that are hard to match or explain against real objects, are often seen about 11.30 p.m.

TROUT INN, BICKLEIGH

Having written and researched a book on Bickleigh, and its immediate area, one thing that was noticeable was the number of different owners that the Trout Inn has had. Now we are not suggesting, for one moment, that the turnover is anything to do with its ghost, but for such an idyllic spot it's curious that some of its owners haven't kept the pub for long before moving on.

The ghost is that of a former employee, hired for his culinary skills as a chef. Although he has made various appearances the one recorded here relates to 1989 when a new owner, Mr Latham, came face to face with him in the kitchen. It appears that the ghost emerged from a cupboard in the pub's kitchen. He then leant, for several seconds, on a sideboard before fading away into nothingness.

THE WEST COUNTRY INN, NEAR HARTLAND

This former seventeenth century coaching inn is on the busy North Devon/North Cornwall main trunk road, the A39, about a mile from the Cornwall/Devon border. It lies not far from Bursdon Moor, in the heart of some attractive countryside, about three miles south of the village of Hartland.

The rural remoteness of the area led to the situation where post sent to outlying farms had to be collected from this inn by farmers, who would have to look in the window of the inn to see if there was any mail for them. Other farmers seeing post for their neighbours would pass on the message, this type of "Bush-Telegraph" system working quite well in the absence of other forms of communications in those days of yesteryear. This remote inn's history has a bearing on its ghost because, in the past, fairs were held each spring and autumn, the extremes of summer and winter being deemed unsuitable for such gatherings. The fairs were held at the back of the inn and the scene was a colourful one with hill farmers and gypsies mingling to do brisk trade, all in the hope of striking a good deal.

The story is locally told of how an attractive seventeen-year-old girl is lured away by a handsome, swarthy gypsy. However, he is a bad lot and murders the poor girl. She is the one who has returned to haunt the inn and her footsteps have been heard. Any resident dogs have been scared by the ghostly girl, their fur standing up on end when she is around. Guests staying there in the past have also been aware of a presence, at times, the most tangible evidence being curtains drawn at bedtime were pulled back in the morning, nobody admitting to doing this.

Up to the 1970s many people claimed to have seen this young girl but recent sightings have been much more scarce. When former landlord, Alan Higgins, ran the inn, many years ago, his family suddenly noticed footsteps running about upstairs. Suspecting a human intruder was up there, a strategy was quickly hatched to catch them, there being two staircases to the upper storey. Two rolling pins were grabbed for protection and each staircase was covered as the inn's residents gingerly closed in on their unwanted guest. A thorough search ensued as the two parties eventually met up, nobody coming face to face with the ghost of the young girl, this time!

WHITE HART, CULLOMPTON

So what's wrong with Cullompton then for this is yet another haunted tale from a small town where almost every one of its pubs has something spooky to offer.

A secret concealed room was found that had no door but a window, a detail that would have rendered it useless but one that suggests a sinister saga as there is every chance that somebody was walled up here. The window was so designed that people gazing up from ground level couldn't have seen it. However, although it would have been appropriate and convenient for this ghost book if that room had been the haunted one this is not the case. Room 8 is the one that is visited by "Angie" who has made her presence felt on a number of occasions. Nothing is known of "Angie" but she is not alone as other, but anonymous, ghostly children keep her company. They like to play on the landing and are often heard in the small hours of the morning.

We have now travelled alphabetically through some of Devon's pub names. Obviously this is only a selection and it's inevitable that many more pubs will have ghosts – they are all licensed for spirits after all. If your 'local' has an extra resident or two, perhaps not mortal enough to have been accounted for in the last official census but real enough to those who share their premises with them, do let us know. And so, with the spooks all sorted out, for the time being, we can have that much-needed stiff drink before we start on the next 'round' of pub ghosts from Devon …

FURTHER SUGGESTED READING

THE GHOSTS OF EXETER, Sally and Chips Barber
What has Wee Willie Winkie got in common with a nun, monk, highwayman, sailor, devils and sprites? Well, they are all ghostly characters seen by people in Exeter so read this collection of ghostly happenings and discover more about some of Exeter's 'invisible' attractions!

THE GHOSTS OF TORBAY, Deryck Seymour
Do you believe in ghosts? Of course not! What a load of rubbish! Thus Deryck Seymour starts his quest to chronicle the spooky, mysterious, strange and inexplicable ghostly goings-on in Torbay. Ghosts in Torbay are prolific in their range and this book makes fascinating reading, so prepare yourself for a few surprises from a surfeit of spirits!

THE GHOSTS OF BERRY POMEROY CASTLE, Deryck Seymour
Berry Pomeroy Castle – it is regarded as "The Most Haunted Castle in Britain"! Deryck Seymour's fascination with Berry Pomeroy dates back to his childhood and, knowing that he is a great authority on the subject, many people have told him of their experiences ranging from mere bad feelings to outright stark horror. He has now compiled these experiences into this fascinating little book.

THE GHOSTS OF TOTNES, Bob Mann
Totnes is an ancient town full of old buildings. And if Bob Mann is to be believed, there are ghosts crawling out of the woodwork at almost every turn!

THE GHOSTS OF BRIXHAM, Graham Wyley
Graham Wyley has been billed as Britain's Number One Ghostbuster and in this book he has compiled some of his favourite, true haunting experiences from his home town of Brixham.

THE GHOSTS OF PLYMOUTH, Nancy Hammonds
We all know Plymouth is steeped in history – but did you know it is also steeped in ghosts? It has haunted houses, spectral soldiers and sailors, and phantom-infested pubs! Nancy Hammonds has been collecting spooky stories and reports of weird phenomena for many years and has now put together this entertaining collection of true ghost stories as told by local people who have encountered the supernatural.

DARK AND DASTARDLY DARTMOOR, Sally and Chips Barber
Dartmoor is an ancient landscape steeped in a wealth of folklore, legends and ghost stories, some based on fact, others passed on by word of mouth. Read about the Devil and his hounds, headless horses, talking rivers, pigs in wigs, phantom cottages, and examine the unique "Ghost Map of Dartmoor".

GHASTLY AND GHOSTLY DEVON, Sally and Chips Barber
Ghastly and Ghostly Devon is a compilation of gruesome stories and ghastly deeds perpetrated in Darkest Devon. Murderous monks, resurrected rectors, bodies in bogs, craftily concealed corpses, misinformed messiahs and cave-dwelling cannibals are just some of the ghastly and ghostly participants, or victims, included within this book.

WEIRD AND WONDERFUL DARTMOOR, Sally and Chips Barber
Weird and Wonderful Dartmoor is packed with amusing anecdotes and stories, some stranger than fiction, that could only happen in a place like Dartmoor!

HAUNTED HAPPENINGS IN DEVON, Judy Chard
Read about the ghost which hitchhikes along the A38, a garage where spanners fly through the air, a full scale military battle only heard in one hotel room, a spirit which smokes cigars, the ghosts of television and radio, various ghostly pets, and many more amazing and mystifying tales about dreams and premonitions which came true.

MURDERS AND MYSTERIES IN DEVON, Ann James
From The Man They Could Not Hang to the Infamous Baby Murderer of Torquay – Murders always Hit the Headlines! In this intriguing compilation of murders and mysteries from darkest Devon, the author has investigated the most notorious cases alongside some of the less well-known tales, telling the stories in a clear and concise easy-to-read style.

THE GREAT LITTLE CHAGFORD BOOK, Chips Barber
The moorland town of Chagford has long been a popular place to visit and a marvellous one in which to live. The Great Little Chagford Book has been written for all those people who have a special place in their hearts for this inland resort. It features customs and characters, people and pubs, ghost stories and golf courses and much, much more.

A SECRET CIRCLE, Deryck Seymour
Herein lies some lovely countryside, many attractive hamlets and villages and absorbing stories. It is an area rich in history from Ashburton to Newton Abbot and round to Totnes, encompassing Broadhempston and Littlehempston, Ipplepen, Denbury, East and West Ogwell and Staverton.

For a full list of current titles, please send SAE to Obelisk Publications, 2 Church Hill, Pinhoe, Exeter EX4 9ER or telephone (01392) 468556.